DOUGHNUT DANGER

ANTHONY MASTERS

Illustrated by
CHRIS FISHER

KINGFISHER

For Cathy and Tom Maskery with love – A.M.

KINGFISHER
An imprint of Kingfisher Publications Plc
New Penderel House, 283-288 High Holborn
London WC1V 7HZ
www.kingfisherpub.com

This edition published by Kingfisher 2005
First published by Kingfisher 2003
2 4 6 8 10 9 7 5 3 1

A CIP catalogue record for this book
is available from the British Library.

ISBN 0 7534 1139 3

Printed in India
1TR/0505/AJANT/FR(SC)/115SM

Contents

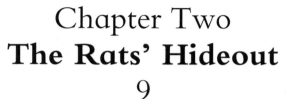

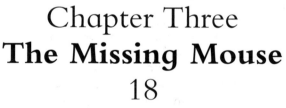

Chapter One
The Rats Are Back

Max Mouse was opening a packet of ring doughnuts.

Mel and Molly were helping him.

"At last," said Max, as the packet split open. "This is the moment we've been waiting for!"

"Yummy," said Mel, biting into
a doughnut.

"Scrummy," squeaked Molly as
she took a nibble.

Suddenly Max stopped eating.

"Did you see that?" hissed Max.

"What?" whispered Molly.

"I thought I saw
a rat's tail."

The three mice looked at each other.

The rats were gangsters. The mice had

had trouble with them before.

Then they heard a horrible sound.

"I know that laugh," Max whispered.

"So do I," said Mel. "That's Ricky Rat."

The laughter was coming from the cellar.

The cellar door was half open.

There was a message pinned next to the door:

The rats are back. Get out while you can! Ricky Rat

"What are we going to do?" asked Mel.
"We've only just moved into this
doughnut factory," said Molly with a sigh.
"And no one's moving us out," said Max.
"Not even Ricky Rat."

Chapter Two
The Rats' Hideout

"We'll have to get rid of the rats," said

Max. "Let's take a look at their hideout

and see what they're up to down there."

The mice crept past the doughnut-

making machine.

The ra...
are bac...
Get out
while you
can!
Ricky
Rat

Mel looked up at it nervously.

The machine was scary in the dark.

10

The mice got to the cellar door.

It was still half open and they could

see a light.

"Be careful. This could be a trap,"

whispered Molly.

"Come on," said Max.

The mice crept down the cellar stairs.

They stopped at the bottom and looked

into the cellar.

Max didn't like what he saw.

Mel and Molly didn't like

what they saw either.

There was one electric light bulb

hanging over a pool table.

The rat gang were having a game.

"My shot," said Ricky.

He pushed Ronnie Rat out of the way

with his pool cue.

Ronnie fell over.

He knocked over some

pots of custard filling.

Custard spilled all over the floor
and all over Ronnie.

The rest of the rat gang laughed.

"Let's get out of here!" said Max.

He quickly ran up the stairs.

Molly was close behind him.

Mel turned round to follow.

But he slipped on some custard

and slid right under the pool table.

"Looks like we've got mice,"

sneered Ronnie.

"You're right, Ronnie," said Ricky.

"And we know how to deal with mice!"

Chapter Three
The Missing Mouse

Max and Molly ran out of the cellar

and hid behind some bags of sugar.

"Where's Mel?" asked Molly.

"I thought he was behind you," said

Max. "He must still be in the cellar."

Max and Molly were afraid.
But they had to find Mel.
They crept down the
cellar stairs again.

"No," squeaked Molly.
"I don't believe it."

Mel was wearing a blindfold.

The rats had put a broom handle
over a big vat of jam.

They were making Mel walk the plank!

Ronnie was standing on a pile of boxes
next to the vat.

"Start walking!" he ordered.

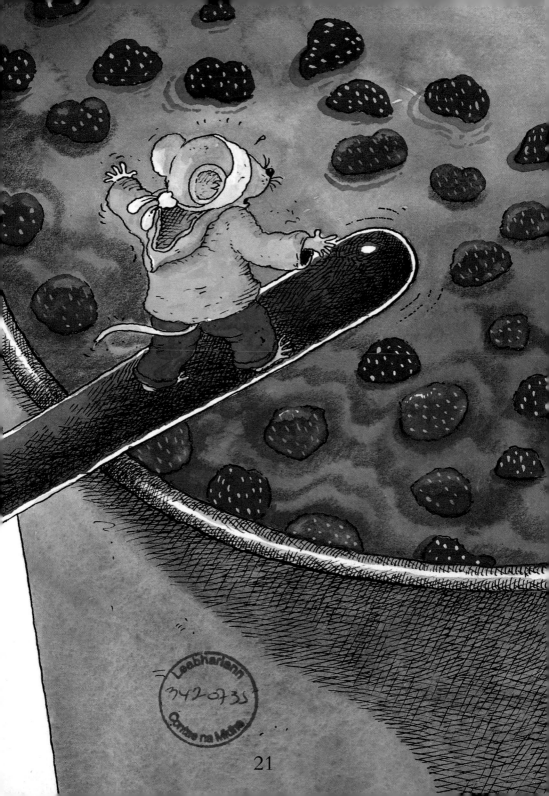

"What are we going to do?" whispered Molly.

"I'm going to rescue Mel," said Max. There were some shelves behind the vat of jam. Max ran over to them. So far none of the rats had seen him.

Max climbed up onto
the shelves.

"There's another mouse!"
Ronnie shouted, jumping
down from the boxes.

"Get him!" yelled Ricky.

But Max was too fast.

Max jumped onto the broom handle.

Mel was too frightened to move.

Max pulled off Mel's blindfold.

"Quick!" he shouted as he pulled Mel

onto the edge of the vat. "Jump!"

The two mice jumped down and raced

across the floor.

Ronnie tried to jump too, but he lost

his balance and fell into the vat of jam.

"Help!" Ronnie shouted, as he splashed about in the jam.

The rats stared over the edge of the vat.

"You idiot!" said Ricky.

He turned to the other rats.

"Get Ronnie out of there!" he shouted.

"Then follow me. We're going to get those mice!"

Chapter Four
Max Has a Plan

Max, Mel and Molly met up behind
a big bag of flour.

"That was close," gasped Molly.

"We need to get rid of those rats,"
said Max. "And I think I know just
how we can do that."

He began to whisper to Molly and Mel.

The rats were looking for the mice.

Ronnie was making squelching sounds as he walked. He was still covered in jam.

Max jumped out from behind the bag
of flour.

"Come and get me!" he squeaked.

"Don't worry," hissed Ricky. "We'll

get you all right."

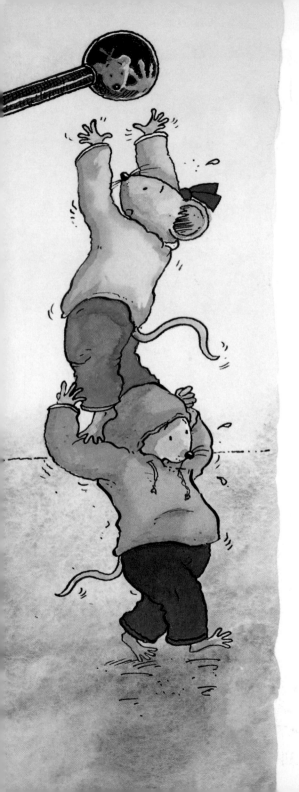

While the rats
were chasing Max,
Mel and Molly
tiptoed under the
doughnut-making
machine.
"Bend down so
I can get up on
your shoulders,"
whispered Molly.
Mel began to
wobble.
"You're too
heavy," he
squeaked.
"I can't hold you."

"If I can just reach the switch," said
Molly, "I can get the conveyor belt
moving. Then Max can take those rats
for a ride."

But Mel was really wobbling now.
The two mice ended up in a heap on
the floor.

Max was running in circles.

He was getting very tired.

Ricky and his rat gang were starting

to catch up with him.

Max felt a nasty nip on his tail

several times.

What are Mel and Molly doing? he

wondered. *Why don't they hurry up?*

Molly climbed onto Mel's
shoulders again.
Mel tried hard not to wobble.
Molly reached up
towards the switch.
"I can't hold on
much longer,"
Mel gasped.
"Nearly got it,"
said Molly, as she
reached up higher.

At last, there was a click as she pulled the switch down.

The machine made a loud clanking sound and started making doughnuts.

Chapter Five
A Sticky End

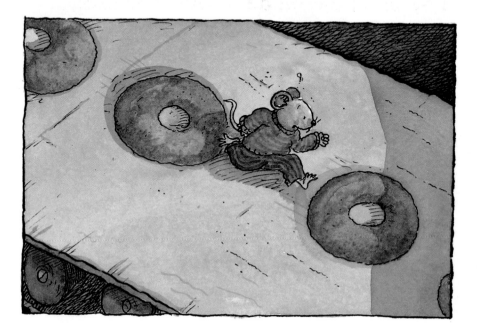

The conveyor belt was moving.

Max jumped onto it.

Ricky and the rat gang were close
behind him.

Freshly made doughnuts were coming
out of the machine.

The doughnuts were heading

towards the packing machine.

So were Max and the rat gang.

Max ran as fast as he could along

the conveyor belt, dodging between

the doughnuts.

The machine began to shower
the doughnuts with sugar.
Max dodged the sugar.
So did the rats.

Then the machine began to squirt icing on the doughnuts.

Max dodged the icing.

But Ronnie got splattered.

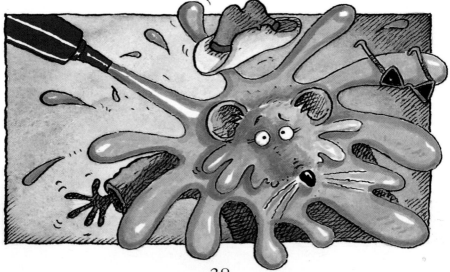

Suddenly the machine was squirting

chocolate.

Max dodged again.

But Ricky was too slow. He got splashed.

Max was well out
in front now.
He could see the
mechanical arms
of the doughnut-
packing machine.
They were
grabbing the
doughnuts and
putting them
into boxes.

DOUGHNUT

Max got ready to jump off.

"Now!" he yelled.

Molly and Mel ran under the machine
and held up a sheet of plastic wrap.

"Here I come!" shouted Max.

He jumped and landed safely on the

plastic wrap.

"Watch out!" yelled Ricky to the

rat gang.

But it was too late.

Max, Molly and Mel were sitting

on top of the packing machine,

nibbling doughnuts.

They watched as boxes of doughnuts

moved along the conveyor belt.

"There they go," said Mel, staring

down at one of the boxes.

Inside each doughnut was a rat.

"They don't look too happy," said Max.

"Bye, bye," squeaked Molly, as the conveyor belt took the box out of the factory. Soon it would be loaded onto a van and taken to the supermarket.

"Those doughnuts are going to be a real surprise," said Mel, licking sugar off his whiskers.

"You bet they are," laughed Max. "They're the first rat-flavoured doughnuts ever made!"

About the Author and Illustrator

Anthony Masters used to run a children's theatre, and also held drama and writing courses in schools and libraries. But he is best known for his own stories for children.
He says, "Rats make brilliant baddies, and the rats in this story are always up to no good.
I think Max Mouse and his friends are really brave to stand up against Ricky and his gang."

Chris Fisher's favourite subject at school was art, and now he is the illustrator of more than 70 books for children. Chris enjoyed inventing all the exciting machines for the mice's doughnut factory home. He says, "I would love to live in a doughnut factory. But I would never get any work done. I would spend all day munching jam doughnuts. Yummy!"

Tips for Beginner Readers

1. Think about the cover and the title of the book. What do you think it will be about? While you are reading, think about what might happen next and why.

2. As you read, ask yourself if what you're reading makes sense. If it doesn't, try rereading or look at the pictures for clues.

3. If there is a word that you do not know, look carefully at the letters, sounds, and word parts that you do know. Blend the sounds to read the word. Is this a word you know? Does it make sense in the sentence?

4. Think about the characters, where the story takes place, and the problems the characters in the story faced. What are the important ideas in the beginning, middle and end of the story?

5. Ask yourself questions like:
Did you like the story?
Why or why not?
How did the author make it fun to read?
How well did you understand it?

Maybe you can understand the story better if you read it again!